How To Individualize Learning

By Alan Gartner and Frank Riessman

Library of Congress Catalog Card Number: 77-089842
ISBN 0-87367-100-7
Copyright © 1977 by The Phi Delta Kappa Educational Foundation
Bloomington, Indiana

TABLE OF CONTENTS

Introduction	7
Learning Styles	9
Cognitive Style and Affective Style	13
Learning by Teaching	16
Moving to Action	18
Poor or Slow?	21
What Teachers Can Do	24
The Student as Producer	27
Conclusion	29

Introduction

No goal of classroom practice is more frequently hailed and less frequently achieved than individualized instruction. A problem in moving from declarations of desire to achievements in practice is that efforts at individualization, for the most part, have been ancillary to other activities. We suggest the combining of three approaches that together would maximize the individualization of instruction. These are: the *diagnostic and prescriptive approach*, attention to the *differing learning styles* of children, and the concept of children *learning by teaching*. Separately, each is directed toward the individualization of learning. In concert, they go beyond the merely additive to the synergistic.

The diagnostic-prescriptive approach builds upon concepts developed in special education. It involves attending to the characteristics (more often weaknesses than strengths—more on this later) of each child and developing an individual plan (prescription). This approach, with its attention to students' needs rather than to predesigned curriculum units, has been increasingly adopted in general education programs; for example, it is a mandatory feature in all Teacher Corps projects and is used as a key instructional strategy by local school districts such as Central Harlem's Community School District 5 in New York City.

As Beth Atwood has shown (see "Helping Students Recognize Their Own Learning Styles," *Learning*, April, 1975), not only do individuals perceive and modify experience in their own unique manner but attention to these differences in learning styles can be the key to independent learning. A decade ago Frank Riessman, in *The Culturally Deprived Child* (and more recently in *The Inner City Child*, Harper and Row, 1976), pointed out the differing learning styles of children and the importance for teachers to build upon the child's special style. And recent neurophysical studies have pointed to the potential for identifying the characteristics of individual brain functions and, thereby, a dimension of the child's cognitive style.

The learning-by-teaching concept builds upon the centuries-old experience that, in the teaching situation, it is the teacher who learns most. Studies of programs sponsored by the National Commission on Resources for Youth, as well as Youth Tutoring Youth programs in hundreds of school systems, have found significant gains, both affective and cognitive, for the children who do the teaching/tutoring. And these gains have been most impressive among children who themselves are having difficulty in school.

Each of these three approaches serves to individualize instruction. Teachers can combine them. Indeed, it is in their combination that the power of each can be magnified.

There is a central concept in achieving this power, well-known but often ignored. That is, it is the student who must do the learning; the role of others can only be to facilitate that learning. In fact, this is a characteristic of all human service work; as one authority put it, in the services the "consumer is producer." For example, the patient in a mental health program is not only the consumer of the service but he must work in achieving the service's goal: his* own mental health. The professional service provider (doctor or other) cannot produce the patient's improved health in the way a factory worker can produce a car, for example. Only the patient himself can do that. Similarly, students are not only consumers of teaching but are the producers of their own learning. Or, as Lady Plowden put it in a report on the British open classroom, "The child is the agent of his own learning." And the more actively engaged the student becomes, the more effective a producer of learning he will become. Individualizing instruction is a way to help that student become a more effective producer of his own learning.

In the following pages we will look briefly at the concepts of learning styles and learning by teaching. Then we will turn to ways of combining them with diagnosis and prescription. We will be particularly concerned with ways of mobilizing the student as a producer of his own learning.

---

*For clarity and economy, we use the masculine form of pronouns throughout this fastback when no specific gender is implied. While we recognize the trend away from this practice, we see no graceful alternative. We hope the reader will impute no sexist motives; certainly no sexism is intended. —*The Editors*

Language, of course, communicates meaning. Thus, our text when describing people did not refer to only those of the male sex. We abhor the decision of the editors in changing that. —*Alan Gartner and Frank Riessman*

Learning Styles

> Some physicists start by concentrating on detail. For myself, I must start not from detail but from a general connection, a feeling I have as about the way things should be.
>
> —Werner Heisenberg

It is not only variations in preferences for starting from the general or the specific which distinguish differing learning styles, but also whether a person learns best from the concrete or from the abstract; whether the learner prefers to work alone or in a group; whether he learns from interchange with others or from books.

And there are those who learn quickly and others who learn slowly. Often, we are inclined to label the latter stupid rather than to see slowness as yet another learning style. A slow learner may simply be extremely careful, meticulous, or cautious. The child may refuse to generalize easily, wanting first to understand the concept in its various parts.

Some children learn more readily by reading, others by hearing. And some learn faster when they can be physically involved in the process, doing things with their hands and bodies.

Some children like to work for long periods on one topic without a break, others to shift back and forth from subject to subject. Some learners take a long time to warm up, while others get into their work very quickly. Some people prefer to sit at a desk, others to walk around. Some need absolute silence, while others can work in a confusion of noise.

Today, it seems, if a child does not learn something right off, we assume that the difficulty must arise from an emotional block or conflict, or a "learning disability." There may be a different way of looking at the problem. Children may not be learning because the instructional approach is not suited to their style, hence they cannot utilize their power effectively. Too often, teachers behave like social workers or psychologists. And, of course, much literature on learning theory relates to animals and molecular concepts. As a recent article in the *Phi Delta Kappan* noted, "students may have emotional or psychological problems that tend to inhibit academic growth, but often they are the *result* of having been required to accommodate to noncomplementary instructional strategies and environments rather than the *cause* of their inability to learn as easily as some of their classmates."

As teachers, we would do better to look to the more wholistic and molar dimensions of learning that operate at the level of behavior. We need to assess whether a child is an aural or visual or physical learner, etc. Moreover, we too often search for a single "best" way, as when we suggest that a child or student "survey the chapter first." Some students cannot do that. They become so anxious or disturbed when asked to take the overall view that they cannot function. They want very much to read a chapter atomistically. It does not help to tell them that they are not proceeding in the right way.

The same argument applies to examinations or tests. For some people a test provides just the right kind of mild anxiety to stimulate the integration of a great deal of material that needs to be learned. On the other hand, there are large numbers of people for whom tests are a terrible experience, causing disorganization and anxiety, thus preventing the student from working. Tests are not adapted to the style of these individuals. When educators argue that tests are marvelous because they aid pupils, providing corrections and criticism, they are referring to persons with a particular style. Undoubtedly tests work well for some pupils, but there are others who forget their wrong answers on tests because it disturbs them too much to remember them.

There is a great deal of controversy in the traditional literature on the very question of whether repression of wrong answers occurs or whether "punishment" for giving the wrong answers on tests helps to produce better recall. We are suggesting that two different styles are involved here. For some people, the information that they gave wrong answers is extremely useful and challenging. If this information is called to their attention in a positive and stimulating way, it makes the wrong answer the figure in the foreground. It draws the incorrect responses to their attention in a constructive manner. For other people, knowing that they have made a mistake is extremely disturbing and destructive of morale; it may lead to repression of the information. Therefore, depending upon one's style and one's way of dealing with these problems, tests may or may not be useful.

In everybody's style there are certain strengths. And everybody has an Achilles' heel. The issue in developing a significant change is related to how one controls the Achilles' heel and how one utilizes the learner's strengths. This is the central problem of the strategy of style.

Although style is individual to the child, we can make some useful generalizations about the cognitive style of inner-city youngsters. The following dimensions seem to characterize many of them:

1. Strong development of nonaural senses such as the visual, tactile, and kinesthetic

2. Well-developed nonverbal forms of communication such as gestures

3. Greater expression in informal, unstructured, spontaneous situations

4. Positive response to learning in cooperative settings such as children teaching children, youth tutoring youth

5. Emphasis on learning from experience and action, and a strong responsiveness to work-study programs, field-based learning, action learning

Inner-city children have considerable facility with informal or public language, and this is expressed best in unstructured, spontaneous situations. They verbalize more freely around action and things they can see. They understand more language than they speak. Their nonverbal forms of expression are highly developed. And they often exhibit imaginative and perceptive word associations.

Anyone who has worked with inner-city children knows that one of the surest ways to involve them in an activity is to make it into a game. Teachers have told about setting up a mock court in the classroom that enabled the class to discuss discipline, justice, and government in a meaningful way. Originally, they had found it difficult to interest the children in these subjects, but the excitement of a make-believe court attracted considerable attention and provided a good beginning for discussion on a higher, more abstract level.

What is the source of the "games" orientation of inner-city children? Apparently, it is related to their down-to-earth, spontaneous approach to things. This extraverbal communication is usually called forth in games, most of which are not work-bound. Also, most games (not all, by any means) are person-centered and generally are concerned with direct action and visible results. Games are usually sharply defined and structured, with clear-cut goals. The rules are definite and can be readily absorbed. The inner-city child enjoys the challenge of the game and feels he can "do" it.

But despite various types of latent creativity, inner-city children often fail to realize their potential because of lack of mastery of standard English. This is their Achilles' heel.

The forms of communication characteristic of inner-city children raise important educational questions. The acquisition of knowledge obviously requires some degree of facility with formal language. Inner-city children are capable of utilizing language in a rich and free fashion, have well-developed, nonverbal ways of communicating, but lack skill in standard English. The problem is how to help them to attain this level of language so that their creative potential can be fully realized.

It would be easy to say, as many have said, that we must give these children what most middle-class parents give their children, i.e., we must stimulate them in the use of language through reading, discussion, and the like. However, it is probable that this alone would not work, nor would it make the best use of the inner-city child's particular mode of functioning. Their nonlinguistic skills should not be ignored or suppressed but brought out and integrated with verbal communication. Thus, it would seem essential that the method of teaching formal language to inner-city children take advantage of their communication style by employing teaching techniques that, as much as possible, stress the visual, the physical, and the active. We must be careful not to try to make these children over into replicas of middle-class children. The educational system should be pluralistic enough, broad enough, to find a place for a variety of learning styles.

Thus, while we must recognize enormous individual differences, it would seem that some basic dimensions characterize the cognitive style of inner-city youngsters, and we must build upon these in the educational program. Inner-city youngsters seem to learn best through games, role playing, doing, seeing, talking, and learning in groups. These strengths can be captured and used to expand reading and writing abilities, without necessarily developing a reading or writing style.

Cognitive Style and Affective Style

A central aspect of a child's learning style is his cognitive style. Since 1972, Oakland Community College personnel have been working in the East Lansing (Michigan) schools to train teachers in skills needed to determine a child's cognitive style.

A child's cognitive style is the way he takes meaning from the world around him, how he comes to know what he knows. The technique used in determining a child's cognitive style is called "mapping." By the use of tests and observations, and in interviews, the teacher seeks answers to the question of how a child derives meaning his own unique way. How does the child note his surroundings, seek meaning, and become informed? Is he a listener or a reader? Does he make up his own mind or seek consensus with his peer groups? Does he think like a mathematician or a news commentator? (From *Teacher Improvement Project*, East Lansing Schools, Michigan.)

The "map" includes how a child uses symbols, the social and cultural determinants that affect him, and the method of the student's thinking. Here are the maps developed for two third-grade students (actually the East Lansing program uses a form of algebraic shorthand developed by Oakland Community College President Joseph E. Hill):

Student Number One

Symbols and Their Meanings	*Cultural Determinants*	*Modalities of Inference*
Processes more information from hearing than from print.	Influenced by associates; sometimes can work independently.	Sees relationships between things; likes examples.
Does well with written math problems.		Compares and contrasts on one-to-one basis.
Knowledge of social and physical distance.		

Student Number Two

Symbols and Their Meanings	*Cultural Determinants*	*Modalities of Inference*
Gets more meaning from written materials than from verbal directions.	Is an individualist; makes up his own mind.	Categorizes and classifies.
Dedicated to a set of rules and principles.	Will take directions from an authority figure.	Makes decisions after carefully considering all available information.
Is able to identify with another person's role.		

Based upon such maps, individualized learning programs can be successfully developed for every student.

We are concerned with going beyond such cognitive mapping in two ways, however. First, to help the individuals become aware of their own styles, strengths, and potentials—because this is the source of individual learning power. And, second, to include in the notion of a child's learning style dimensions beyond the cognitive.

The Learning Style Inventory is a tool which goes beyond the cognitive to four broad sets of influence categories that affect learners: 1) immediate environment (sound, temperature, light, and design); 2) emotionality (motivation, responsibility, persistence, and structure); 3) sociological needs (self, pairs, peers, teams, adults, and/or varied); and 4) physical needs (perceptual strengths and/or weaknesses, time of day, intake of food and fluids, mobility).

One of the central features of a child's affective content is the need for power, i.e., to exhibit strength in ways other than the physical. A Syracuse teacher developed an interesting way for children to feel this type of power. When she worked with a group of seventh-grade children on sentence structure, the youngsters responded that the work was "grade school" and "terrible." She asked them how they thought the grade school kids felt about it, and they were sure it was the same. She suggested visiting the grade school and interviewing the students there. After developing the interview material—a learning activity in itself—the seventh-graders interviewed a class of third-graders (who were pleased with the attention) and armed with their findings, the older students decided to develop "better" materials for the third grade. After feedback from the third-grade youngsters as to the materials, the seventh-grade youths revised the materials and then "taught" them to the younger children. Of course it was the seventh-grade children who had been involved in the most active learning—but this time in learning with a socially valuable purpose—helping the younger children. Also, this learning was self-empowering. (Adapted from *The Disadvantaged: Challenge to Education*, 1968.)

What this Syracuse teacher had done, of course, was to rediscover the power of learning by teaching, in this case cross-age teaching, where older children are given responsibility for teaching younger children.

Learning by Teaching

Playing the role of teacher in a learning-by-teaching program can serve both to help the older child feel a greater sense of his own strength and to learn or relearn school material. Additionally, it can be a way to help children learn about their own learning styles and become self-diagnosticians and prescribers.

The power of learning by teaching comes from several factors, both cognitive and affective. As to the affective domain, we have already noted the importance of the child gaining in self-respect and ego strength. This is particularly important for those youngsters who are doing poorly in school. For example, a Beaverton (Oregon) junior high boy involved in a learning-by-teaching program, although he was doing poorly in school, was teased for carrying a third-grade math book. He proudly retorted that he was the teacher of the third grade!

The self-confidence that is built includes the factor of being singled out, specially chosen; the doing of an important activity; and the developing of competence. And here we can see the interrelationship between the affective and cognitive, with growing mastery in the one arena supporting and reinforcing mastery in the other.

In the cognitive arena, a student learns by reviewing the material and coming to understand it more fully or deeply. While the reviewing may be designed to enable the tutor to present the material better, often the tutor will have to reformulate it so as to help the child better understand it. Already knowing the "facts" of the subject, the student as teacher may be able to grasp the underlying structure, to see problems in new and different ways, to reformulate them, to reconceptualize issues. In sum, the student reviews the material and then has to organize, prepare, and illustrate it to present it to his student; the tutor may seek out the basic character of the subject, its structure, in order to teach it better, and thus may understand it better; the tutor may try to reshape or reformulate it so as to enable the pupil to learn it, and in doing so the tutor may see things in new ways.

In this process of teaching another, especially in the close attending involved in the one-to-one relationship, the tutor has a chance to observe another in the process of learning. Something of this is captured in this log entry of a Portland (Oregon) high school student who was tutoring a grade school girl:

> December 9. All of a sudden Sherry understands division. She was pleasant and cooperative. She was like she used to be. I guess I was wrong about her not trying. She didn't understand and lost confidence. I am sorry I didn't understand the situation. She is a real good kid. I am never going to accuse her again.

The learning-by-teaching program should include a "debriefing" time for the tutors. This time provides an opportunity for the teacher to help the tutors observe and reflect upon the learning process and styles of their pupils. If it is done skillfully (and gently), it also permits the student-tutor to reflect upon his own ways of learning. For the goal here is to enable the tutors to become more aware of differing learning styles and to become conscious of their own learning styles.

Moving to Action

The first aim is to have a person become aware of the strengths and potentials in his style, because this awareness is going to be a source of power. Thus, if an individual has a physical style, he has to learn the special attributes of this style and how to use them. Youngsters who like to learn by listening and speaking (aural-oral style) are unlikely to change completely and become readers. This is not to suggest that such pupils will fail to learn to read and write fluently. It does suggest that their best learning, the long-lasting, deep learning that gets into their nervous system, may derive from speaking and hearing.

Take an illustration of a different type: A youngster tells us that he sits down to work but cannot concentrate. It is extremely important at this point (and this is crucial in the diagnosis of style) to ascertain as precisely as possible what takes place in this youngster's routine. For example, when does he study?

He may say:

> I come home, throw down my books, and then I start to remember that I have to do some work. So I get out my books. I try to work. I take out the book, but my mind wanders. I look at the book; I look away. I can't get into the work, and after a few minutes of trying this, I begin to feel discouraged; I begin to feel bad. I feel I can't work. I'm no good. I get very worried, and then I run away from the work.

There are many possible explanations for this kind of behavior. One possibility is that this youngster has a slow warm-up period. He does not easily get into something new; he does not shift from whatever he's been doing before (whether he's been outside playing ball or inside listening to the radio). This may be because he is a physical learner. If he is a physical learner, in order for learning to take place he must be involved physically in the work process. He has to get his muscles into it. And this takes time. If this is our student's pattern, then he must come to understand that although he is slow to warm up, this is not necessarily a negative quality; it is simply a different way of approaching work.

Actually, learning for this student may very often be connected with perseverance, once he gets involved. Once he is immersed, he may go deeper and deeper and not be able to shift away from the work easily. The inability to shift doesn't then operate as a negative feature but as a positive element in his style.

But the youngster described here rarely gets to this point. It's not that he doesn't persevere somewhere, in baseball or elsewhere. In his school work he's never gotten past the point of the slow warm-up. He usually schedules his time so that he works for one hour. That doesn't succeed, because it takes him half an hour to warm up. Even if he were to be successful and stick with it for the half hour as a result of a teacher's or guidance worker's support and stimulation, the problem of having only a short time left to work would remain at the end of the half hour. Consequently he has to plan a longer time period of work and recognize in advance that it will take him about half an hour to warm up. In other words, the person who would help our student must give him a definition of his work pattern before he can realize the positive potentialities in it.

When this new definition is provided, it is probable that a number of consequences will follow. Over a period of time the warm-up period will shorten, because part of the difficulty in the long warm-up is the anxiety that emerges. As an individual works, his anxiety decreases and his interest has a chance, concomitantly, to increase.

Another example is one in which a person's strengths are used to deal with his weaknesses. How do you teach people how to read when reading is not their basic style? Everyone is going to need reading ability and writing ability, of course, regardless of his style. In order to teach reading to youngsters for whom it is stylistically uncongenial, a teacher may want to use role playing, which is directly related to the action style of the individual. Students can read about something that they have just role played, or they can read about a trip they have recently taken. While teaching reading under these conditions, teachers must remember that they are not developing a reading style; they are developing a skill, a balance in the pupil's style. The child is developing minimal efficiency in an area that is not rooted in the learner's style. In a sense, the teacher is going after the Achilles' heel—the weakness, the reading difficulty—by developing it through the student's strength, whether it be visual, aural, physical, or whatever. This is a basic tactic for defeating or limiting the weakness: connect it and subject it to the strengths.

Poor or Slow?

An interesting confusion prevails in education circles between the "poor learner" and the "slow learner." The two are assumed to be identical. But need this be so? In a pragmatic culture such as ours, oriented toward quantity, speed, and measurement, this error is easily made. In the classroom it is particularly easy to believe that the child who learns the lesson quickly is a better learner than one who takes a long period of time. But the problem is more complicated than that. The child who learns history more slowly is likely to be ignored and, unwittingly, to be discouraged by teachers. Even if they give him special attention, teachers may reflect their implicit assumption that the child is a poor student. They may demand less of the child, for example. The point is that they never see the slowness as simply another style of learning with potential strengths of its own; nor do they see potential weaknesses (not necessary weaknesses) in the fast learner, who may become glib or impatient with tasks requiring protracted attention. Because of the treatment they receive in the school system, slow learners may then become poor learners.

It is time to put an end to the negative connotation of the term "slow" in the learning process. Slowness can reflect many things. It can indicate caution, a desire to be very thorough, a meticulous style, or great interest that may constrain one to avoid rushing through a problem. Or it may indicate a desire to mull things over. (It may also indicate intellectual inadequacy, of course.)

Extreme slowness probably does connote inadequacy in the absence of counter-indications. Even here we have to be very careful to check all possible blocks, not just the obvious emotional disturbances. There may be auditory blocks, reading diffficulties (not of emotional origin), antagonism to the teacher, etc.

The nature of the slowness itself also has to be carefully examined. A delayed end product does not necessarily mean a slow process of thinking. Because children take a long time to arrive at an answer does not mean that their thinking is retarded. It may be that their thinking is more circuitous, that they are easily distracted, that they will not venture an answer until certain. There are a host of other possibilities.

While our middle-class culture (and the tests it uses) emphasizes speed, there is really no reason to assume that gifted, creative people have to learn rapidly or perform rapidly. We have to become accustomed to the idea of a slow gifted child. Some people take a long time to learn basic concepts, but when they finally do so, they may use the ideas in a thoughtful, penetrating fashion. Others may learn a concept rapidly and then switch to some other area without ever pursuing the concept in depth. There are many slow people who only demonstrate their intellectual power on tasks in which they were slow to take an interest, tasks which have no time requirements. We all know students whose grades were low but who performed quite brilliantly on particular problems or in subjects in which they were deeply immersed. Their poor averages were simply a reflection of the pace required in a school not attuned to their style of work. They often fail in tasks they could handle extremely well if given more time.

Children who are slow to start the study of a topic may benefit from what is called "intensive education," where a subject is studied throughout the day for a period of weeks. (This in contrast to the "concurrent" pattern of junior and senior high school with five or six subjects each day.) Intensive education has been adopted by many colleges, often in an intensive "winterm" in January, and even by some as the mode of instruction for the entire year. Increasingly, high schools are experimenting with such designs.

A recent study of intensive education (*edc. news*, Fall, 1976, 1-3) identifies issues concerning human relationships, the teaching and learning process, and appropriateness. As to human relationships, the more intensive involvement of teacher and students produces both positive and negative experiences. The study reports closer personal relationships between teachers and students, each becoming more "human" and showing moods, weaknesses, enthusiasms. Also, there is better communication and closer relationships among students. Students in intensive education programs begin to help each other informally both in and out of class.

The processes of teaching and learning necessarily are different in an intensive situation. There are greater opportunities for children and teachers to pursue tangents, to relate to their own interests, to dig deeply into the subject. Also, there are greater opportunities for non-school-bound learning activities; for example, an environmental science class can visit a tidal pool without concern about the students missing French. The intensive design gives students greater opportunities to learn something, try it out, and then reflect upon the experience.

The appropriateness of intensive education can be thought of in terms of subject matter, teachers, and students. The study reports both positive and negative experiences with the same subject matter; in other words, there seems to be no subject matter which is automatically "right" or "wrong" for intensive education. For teachers, intensive education requires much more flexibility, planning, and individualization. For some it may be desirable simply as a change of pace, a way of trying something new. So too for students, intensive education may provide a change of pace, a new mode. The study notes that students report that intensive education required greater self-discipline.

We began this discussion of "intensive education" in talking about the student who required a long warm-up. For such children, and others, intensive education may be efficacious. But just as the common concurrent education does not serve all children well, intensive education is not appropriate for all children. We should not tip the scale the other way. Rather, we need to develop opportunities for all youngsters to learn in modes that best fit their styles.

What Teachers Can Do

Achieving this individualization requires much from teachers. Among the teacher variables which affect the establishment of individualized learning situations are the teacher's

1. Personality
2. Teaching style
3. Ability and willingness to learn, risk, change, and grow
4. Awareness of his own unique learning style, so that he may recognize that others learn differently
5. Willingness to evaluate his personal teaching style, techniques, and methods for effectiveness with different kinds of learners
6. Ability to become a co-learner with students

This last variable has broad consequences. A teacher with the ability to become a co-learner appears to students in a role other than that of a "know it all." If part of the teacher's learning involves learning from and with the students, he demonstrates respect for them. When in the learner role, the teacher has a chance to model desirable learner behavior. Normally, of course, the teacher only models teacher behavior, and students are left to discover for themselves desirable and desired learner behavior.

Something of the pattern of teacher activities leading to a learning situation that emphasizes individualization is expressed in the following table. The authors contrast a "developmental" curriculum with a "structured" curriculum.

Characteristics of a Structured vs. a Developmental Curriculum*

Structured Curriculum

1. Coverage
   a. It is comprehensive.
   b. It is able to be planned.
   c. It is predictable.
   d. Deliberate effort is required for integration with the field.
   e. It may or may not account for students' prior knowledge and/or immediate interest.

2. Content
   a. Boundaries are set.
   b. Theory is logically developed.
   c. Student understanding and retention are primarily cognitively-based.
   d. It is course-related.

3. Teacher
   a. He can limit teaching to what he knows.
   b. He can be a directive leader.

4. Process
   a. It is teacher dominated and relies on student cooperation.
   b. A contract is predetermined.
   c. There is variable student participation.
   d. Conformity is frequently the norm.
   e. Motivation is more likely to be derived extrinsically.
   f. Focus is on mastery of content.
   g. Teaching/learning are primarily deductive.

Developmental Curriculum

1. Coverage
   a. It is in-depth with a possibility of gaps.
   b. It is timely.
   c. It is relatively unpredictable.
   d. The content flows naturally to and from field experience.
   e. Students' prior knowledge and/or immediate interest are considered relevant.

2. Content
   a. Boundaries are open.
   b. Theory is built piecemeal.
   c. Student understanding and retention are experientially- and cognitively-based.
   d. It is problem- and issue-related.

3. Teacher
   a. He may require outside expertise.
   b. He is concerned with enabling leadership.

4. Process
   a. It is collegial and relies heavily on student initiative.
   b. A contract is negotiated.
   c. There is strong student participation.
   d. Risk taking is positively reinforced.
   e. Motivation is more likely to be intrinsic.
   f. The focus is on learning how to learn.
   g. Teaching/learning are primarily inductive.

---

*Revised and adapted from "Student Centered Teaching," *Journal of Education for Social Work*, Fall, 1976.

A study* comparing perceptions of individual students and their teachers concerning the youngsters' learning styles (using the Learning Style Inventory) yielded interesting results. While there was high congruence concerning most of the environmental and physical factors, disagreements were greater between teacher and student perceptions as to the students' preferences concerning emotional and sociological needs. Particularly limited was agreement concerning perceptions of self-motivation and persistence. As the authors note, "It may be that students do try, but they become relatively 'unmotivated' and less than persistent (in their teachers' views) because they are incapable of exerting continuous effort toward learning when the style in which they are required to achieve does not complement their own learning style preferences."

---

*Rita Dunn, Kenneth Dunn, and Gary E. Price, "Diagnosing Learning Styles," *Phi Delta Kappan* (January, 1977): 418-420.

The Student as Producer

Each of the activities we have discussed—diagnosis and prescription, awareness of different learning styles, learning by teaching, a developmental curriculum—can contribute to the individualization of learning. Each is within the province of the teacher's responsibility. Now, we shall take the process a step further, for our goal is not only to have students learn better in situations structured by teachers but also in those that are unstructured. We seek, also, the opportunity for students to be self-directed and self-motivated—indeed, self-propelled learners.

For this to be achieved, we need not only teacher diagnosis and prescription, teacher awareness of a child's learning style(s), and so forth, but self-diagnosis and prescription, and awareness of one's own learning style(s).

Beth Atwood has developed some valuable classroom techniques for furthering students' awareness of their own learning styles. She asks students to survey their own ways of learning.

The surveys include some of the following items:

I am most alert for learning new things in the: 1) early morning, 2) midday, 3) late afternoon, or 4) evening.

The easiest way(s) for me to learn something is to : 1) read it, 2) hear it, 3) see it in pictures, 4) try it, 5) write it in my own words, 6) explain it to someone else, or 7) draw a diagram or picture of it.

The kinds of learning situations that bother me most are: 1) large-group sessions, 2) small-group sessions, 3) using learning games such as spelling bees, 4) working with a partner the teacher chose for me, 5) working with a partner who chose me, 6) working with a partner I don't know, 7) working by myself, 8) working on team projects, 9) working in a very quiet place, 10) working in a very noisy place, 11) being interrupted while I'm working, 12) having to take a break in the middle of my work, 13) having to stop when I'm not finished, or 14) having nothing to do while I wait for others to finish.

We have earlier noted the technique of "cognitive style mapping." As developed at Oakland Community College it is a technique counselors use in designing learning modes for students. In what might be described as a participatory diagnosis and prescription, the student would come to learn how to develop his own map—the diagnosis, and how to develop a learning program best suited to his style(s) and need(s). The student, then, becomes the architect of his own learning. He is not working alone but as the key assessor of the needs and developer of the plans.

Conclusion

The goals we have put forth are those that school people have long espoused. Schools have always declared their intent to enable students to *become* strong, self-directed learners. We propose, then, that to achieve these goals schools provide opportunities for their students to *be* strong, self-directed learners.

To do this will require changes in schools, in teachers, and in pupils. Much can be done within the framework of present school organization, although more may be achieved with the adoption of alternatives incorporated in Mario Fantini's concept of "public schools of choice." Similarly, teachers with traditional ideas can recognize that children are different, learn differently, and that their differences need to be recognized. It is not a radical concept to focus upon a child's strengths and to build upon them rather than to emphasize weaknesses and deficits.

The most difficult changes may be those required of the students, for they are being asked to change from passive recipients of someone's teaching to active producers of their own learning. Perhaps what is called for is training in how "to student," to invent a phrase.*
Not only do pupils need to learn about their rights and responsibilities, they also need to learn about how to identify their own learning style(s), to recognize their strengths and weaknesses, to learn how to build upon the former and to overcome the latter, indeed how to use the former to overcome the latter. In effect, students need to learn how to learn both as a means to master the material of the school and as the central consequence of schooling.

---

*As part of a project supported by the Office of Consumers' Education, U.S. Office of Education, we are developing programs designed to help pupils in more effectively playing the student role.